Copyright © 2023 by Hannah Bricknell

All rights reserved. No part of this book may be reproduced in any manner whatsoever without written permission except in the case of brief quotations embodied in critical articles and reviews.

First Printing, 2023

Do you want to learn to draw Jenny Penny and her Friends? This book will show you how.

Did you know your body creates muscle memory?

This means your muscles will start to remember what you are drawing, even if you start by tracing instead of drawing. The lines in this book should be dark enough for you to see them through a blank piece of paper so you can first try tracing them before you draw solo.

Basic Shapes of drawing

Everything that you will draw starts out with basic shapes of circles, squares, triangles, ovals, and rectangles. The book will show you what shapes to start with to draw the characters in this book including all the animals. Circles can connect moving body parts like shoulders, knees, elbows, wrists, and ankles.

Meet Jenny Penny

This character starts with a circle for the head but also for the hat she will wear and for her Magnifying glass. Draw along with me:

Step 1	Step 2	Step 3
Step 4	Step 5	Step 6

And now let me introduce you to the character that started it all. Apple the elephant, he is so cute, isn't he?

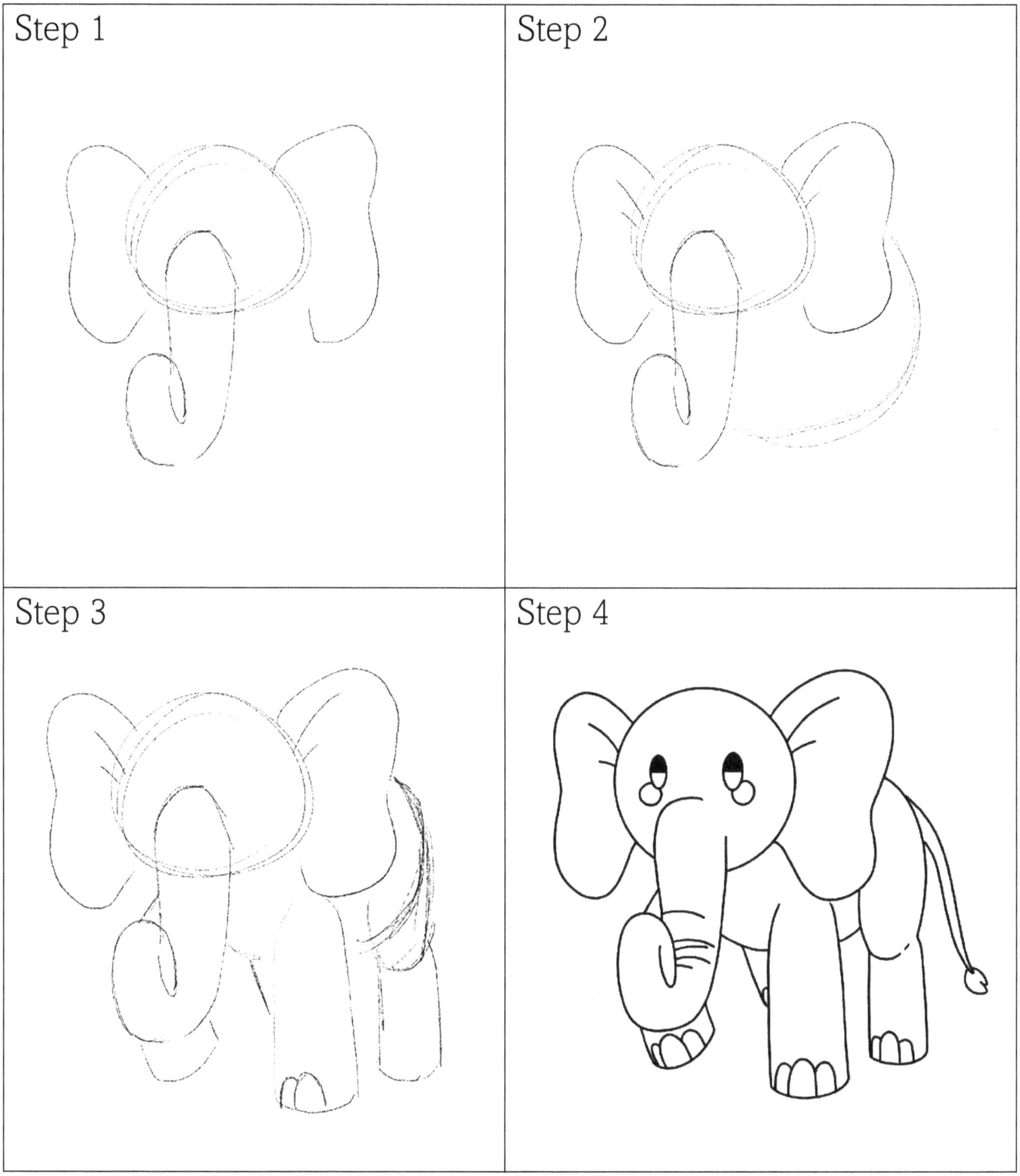

Step 1	Step 2
Step 3	Step 4

Meet Jenny Penny's Mom, she is so nice, and she loves how big her daughter's imagination is when she sees new things.

Step 1

Step 2

Step 3

Meet the Policeman, he helps find out why Apple is there.

Step 1

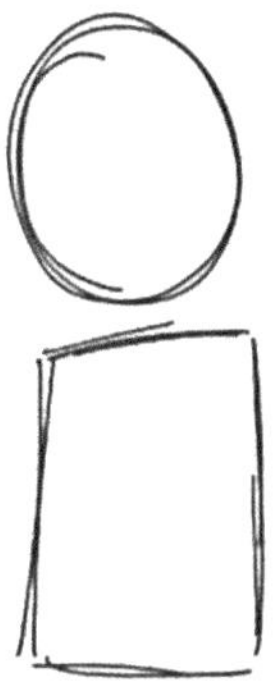

Step 2

Step 3

Here is the Zookeeper. I like his funny hat, don't you?

Step 1	Step 2

Step 3

This is Jenny Penny's House for you to color

Look at what Jenny Penny found! A cute little grasshopper.

Continue drawing what Jenny Penny bonked her head on.

What did Jenny Penny find? Well, an Elephant I do believe.

Do you think Jenny Penny's Mom is surprised to see an Elephant?

What do you think Jenny Penny is telling her dad about?

What do you think the three are talking about in this picture?

Guess what the police officer found?

It is hard to let good things go, isn't it?

Mom and baby Elephant reunited, should they be the same color?

What should her hat say? You decide.

Make more people in the crowd if you want, it is your story!!

Can you also fix Apple's ear?

Acknowledgements

I would like to thank Mauro Azzano who taught me that daring to dream and achieve those goals is doable in publishing.

I would also like to thank my mom for guiding me through this creative publishing process, and to my dad for his support.

Last of all, thank you to my patrons for purchasing this book so that more young people around the world can learn how to draw.

For my latest works, please visit my Instagram page.

H.B. ORIGINALS

www.ingramcontent.com/pod-product-compliance
Lightning Source LLC
Chambersburg PA
CBHW042037100526
44587CB00030B/4471